D0493085

9112000173190

WAR IN THE TRENCHES

Remembering World War One

Peter Hicks

WAYLAND

First published in 2013 by Wayland
Copyright © Wayland 2013

Wayland
338 Euston Road
London NW1 3BH

Wayland Australia
Level 17/207 Kent Street
Sydney, NSW 2000

Editor: Annabel Stones
Designer: Elaine Wilkinson
Researchers: Laura Simpson and Edward Field
at The National Archives

The National Archives, London, England.
www.nationalarchives.gov.uk

The National Archives looks after the UK government's historical documents. It holds records dating back nearly 1,000 years from the time of William the Conqueror's Domesday Book to the present day. All sorts of documents are stored there, including letters, photographs, maps and posters. They include great Kings and Queens, famous rebels like Guy Fawkes and the strange and unusual – such as reports of UFOs and even a mummified rat!

Material reproduced courtesy of The National Archives: p.4 (bottom left): RAIL 253/516 (10) Pvt RAW Dyer; p.5 (bottom): RAIL 253/516 Sgt E F Henderson, and others Army Service Corps 916; p.6 (top): WO 153/1050 (5) Sketch of trenches held by 29th Indian Brigade; p.6 (bottom): WO 95/3911 (1) Sections of various trenches in the Aisne position; p.8 (top): RAIL 253/516 Illustration of men in the trenches; p.8 (bottom): WO 95/391 (1) Sections of various trenches in the Aisne position; p.10 & p.11: ZPER 34/146 Annotated image of British First World War soldier, Illustrated London News, 1915; p.13 (top): RAIL 253/516 (2) Christmas and New Year card from the Front; p.14 (top): RAIL 253/516 Hut accommodation at the Front; p.14 (bottom): ZPER 34/146 Annotated image of British First World War soldier, Illustrated London News, 1915; p.17 (bottom): WO 95/3925 (1) Ferozepore Brigade - Instructions regarding hygiene in trenches; p.18 (top): WO 95/3911 (2) Sections of various trenches; p.20 (top): CAB 45/154 Extract from battle report during the second Battle of Ypres, 1915; p. 23 (middle): ZPER 34/148 Red Cross Workers; p.23 (bottom): RAIL 227/436 (1) Ambulance Train in France; p.24 (main): WO 95/3911 Map of Area La Bassee, 25 October 1914; p.25 & back cover (top): RAIL 253/516 (1) Sapper F H Ferdinand Railway Transport section; p.26 (top): EXT 1/315 The Big Push poster; p.27 (top): EXT 1/315 1 of 2 German trenches before bombardment; p.27 (middle): EXT 1/315 2 of 2 German trenches after bombardment; p.28: RAIL 253/516 Private E Giles, right, with members of his unit; p.29 & back cover (bottom): RAIL 253/516 Sgt Jack Symons KRR; p.33: RAIL 1020/14/11; p.34 (top): WO 32/5484 Ten Australian deserters; p.35 (top): WO 32/5460 (2) Protest against Field Punishment; p.35 (middle): WO 32/5460 (1) Field punishment; p.37: RAIL 253/516 Cartoon XXth Light Division 'A Few Days Rest in Billets'; p.38 (left): RAIL 253/516 Revue programme cover 'Other Days' with the Joystickers; p.38(right): FO 383/196 Jack Harris, music hall comedian and entertainer; p.39 (top): FO 383/196 Jack Harris's Pierrot Troupe; p.39 (middle): RAIL 253/516 (2) J H Hyam and 11th Hussars Football Team; p.39 (bottom): RAIL 253/516 (3) letter 1 of 4, 03-08-1915; p.40 (top left): FO 383/413 (4) French and British POWs arrive at camp from the front, World War I; p.40 (bottom right): FO 383/413 (45) One day's POW parcels, World War I; p.41: FO 383/413 (40) POW football match; p.42: MUN 5/394 (24) Tank experiments; p.43 (middle right): WORK 21/74 (7) Victory Parade London; p.43 (bottom): WORK 21/74 (8) Victory Parade London.

Picture credits: Commonwealth War Graves Commission: p.45 (top). Getty Images: p.7 IWM via Getty Images; p.9 Popperfoto; p.15 (bottom) Popperfoto. Mary Evans Picture Library: p.31 Robert Hunt Collection; p.36 ©The Howells WWI Collection. Peter Hicks: p.45 (middle). Shutterstock: p.15 (top); p.18; p.20 (bottom); p.21; p.22; p.23 (top); p.26 (bottom); p.32; p.34 (bottom); p.44. Wayland: front cover photographs left, right & centre, p.1, pp.2-3, p.4 (map), p.5 (map), pp.12-13, p.16, p.19, p.43 (top).

Background and graphic elements courtesy of Shutterstock.

Disclaimer: Every effort has been made to trace the copyright holder but if you feel you have the rights to any images contained in this book then please contact the publisher.

Please note:
The website addresses (URLs) included in this book were valid at the time of going to press. However, because of the nature of the Internet, it is possible that some addresses may have changed, or sites may have changed or closed down since publication. While the author and publishers regret any inconvenience this may cause to the readers, no responsibility for any such changes can be accepted by either the author or the publishers.

A cataloguing record for this title is available at the British Library.

ISBN 978 0 7502 7841 6

Dewey Number 940.4'1-dc23

Printed in China

Contents

Opening Moves

The causes of World War I (1914–18) are very complicated. In 1914, Europe was split into two rival groups; the 'Triple Entente', consisting of Great Britain, France and Russia, and the 'Triple Alliance', made up of Germany, Austria-Hungary and Italy. Many countries were afraid that others were becoming more powerful. Germany feared encirclement because she was surrounded by France and Russia. A political crisis that summer led to Germany invading Belgium to attack France. Britain, an ally of France and a supporter of Belgian neutrality, declared war on Germany on 4 August.

By 1914, the great powers of Europe were divided into two groups:

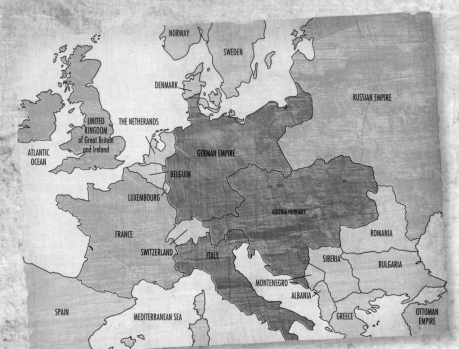

| | Triple Alliance (the Central Powers) | | Triple Entente (the Allies) |

The war begins

The tiny British Army — the British Expeditionary Force (BEF) — at the time only about 150,000 strong, crossed the channel to Belgium and fought with the French to stop Germany taking Paris. They were nearly surrounded and defeated at the town of Mons, but retreated to safety and later joined up with the French at the River Marne in September. The Germans were stopped at this battle and never took Paris.

Private Dyer was in the 2nd Battalion, Bedfordshire Regiment, 47th Division of the BEF.

Stalemate

That autumn both sides tried to out-flank (go round the side of) each other but failed when they reached the North Sea coast. The war had become a stalemate with both sides facing each other along a 300-kilometre front. The British faced the Germans from the North Sea, through Belgium, to the River Somme, while their allies, the French, faced the Germans from the River Somme to the Swiss border.

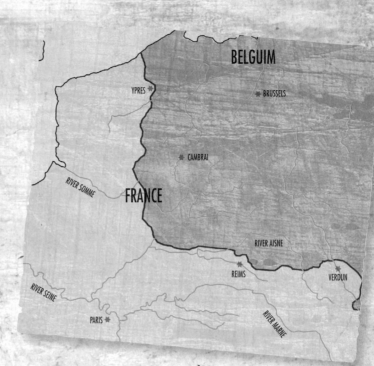

BELGUIM

YPRES
BRUSSELS
CAMBRAI
RIVER SOMME
FRANCE
RIVER AISNE
REIMS
VERDUN
RIVER SEINE
PARIS
RIVER MARNE

■ Under control of Entente forces (Allies)

■ Under control of the Triple Alliance (Central Powers)

The trenches

Both sides dug in to hold their positions and to protect themselves from murderous machine-gun fire and artillery. At first isolated fox-holes were joined up and then, in time, a complicated network of front-line, support and reserve trenches were constructed. The early war of movement was over. The static war, where soldiers would fight from holes in the ground, had begun.

Members of the Army Service Corps, who provided supplies and transport for the troops.

Trenches: The Theory

Trenches were not new for the British Army. They had been used in the Boer War in South Africa (1899–1902) but then they had been temporary defences. What was new about the trenches of 1914–15 was the fact that they were permanent fortifications that men would live and fight in for long periods of time.

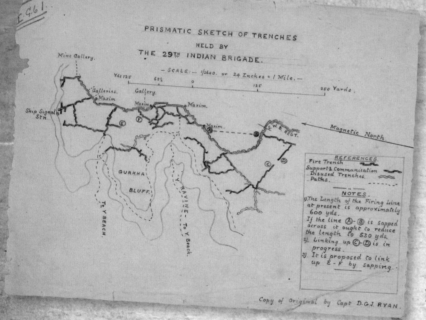

Sketch of the early trench system held by the 29th Indian Brigade.

The front line

A typical stretch of front line consisted of the fire trench from which soldiers could shoot at the enemy. Behind this was a support trench and further back a reserve trench. You entered these lines of trenches through communication trenches at right angles to them. A trench was supposed to be at least one-and-a-half to two metres deep, but because of variations in the soil, they were often shallower which meant soldiers – especially tall ones – had to stoop low or risk injury or death from snipers.

Building trenches

The trenches were dug by the soldiers, who were equipped with shovels. When they dug out the earth they placed some at the front of the trench (called the parapet) and some at the back (the parados) for protection. These banks of earth would be strengthened with sandbags. The space between the Allied and German trenches was called no man's land because neither side owned it. It was very dangerous to attempt to enter it in broad daylight.

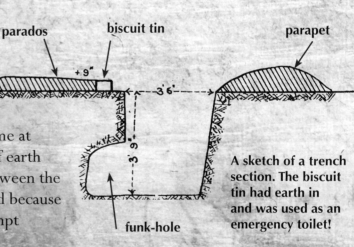

A sketch of a trench section. The biscuit tin had earth in and was used as an emergency toilet!

Fortresses

Fire trenches were never dug straight but in zig-zags or a series of right angles. This was done for protection, to prevent enemy soldiers from firing down the length of the trench and to reduce the effects of blast from exploding shells. The zig-zags were called traverses or fire-bays and as well as giving protection they allowed soldiers to fire at the enemy from different angles. These positions were difficult to attack because of the sharp barbed-wire placed in front of them. The trenches had become fortresses!

"...had a dirty time yesterday morning dodging ...bombs. They can be seen descending through the air and then a scoot is made round the corner."

A SOLDIER DESCRIBES THE DANGERS OF ARTILLERY.

Soldiers of the King's Liverpool Regiment check a map of the trenches.

Trenches: In Practice

When a battalion (1007 men) was sent to the front line, it would expect to spend about two weeks in a fire trench, a week in support, two weeks in reserve and one week resting out of the line. However, because of local conditions and troop shortages, it was sometimes much longer...

Cushy enough!

The battalion was divided into companies (227 men) and platoons (52 men) and each platoon was made up of four sections of 13 men. Each section had to look after a sector of fire trench and was led by a corporal. When men took over a new sector – usually at night – the troops being relieved were always asked, "What's it like here?" The answer was always, "Cushy enough!" meaning soft or easy. This was not always true!

Cheery troops in a freezing trench. This was a Christmas card for families back home, but the reality was miserable.

Digging in

When the soil was reasonably dry, the trench was dug out and a firm fire-step was cut. From here, soldiers could either observe no man's land or shoot at the enemy. However, when the soil was very wet, as it was in Belgium, any excavation soon filled up with water. The trenches had to be built up above ground-level with sandbags and wood, known as breastworks.

parados

parapet

+ 1'

+ 9"

– 3'

– 1'

– 6"

– 3.9'

– 4.9'

– 6"

The sides of trenches and fire steps were strengthened with wood or corrugated iron.

More water

Rain was a major problem because water ran down to the floor of the trench and quickly turned to mud. Continuous rain meant the sides of the trench were weakened, so a lot of time had to be spent repairing and reinforcing them. This was not an easy job in wet and muddy conditions. The situation was made worse by the constant enemy artillery barrages. If a shell landed in or near a trench it could easily collapse on to the defenders, often burying them alive. If they were not dug out quickly, they could suffocate.

A British soldier stands in a flooded trench in Belgium.

A CORPORAL WRITES HOME IN FEBRUARY 1916.

"...off to these trenches, which are in the Ypres district. The trenches here are in very bad condition, mud and water up to the knees and over."

Routine

What was the daily routine like for soldiers in the front line? An hour before dawn, any sleeping soldiers were woken up, ordered to 'fix bayonets' and stand on the fire-step. This was called the morning 'stand to' and was designed to watch for any early enemy activity.

Keeping clean

It was essential to keep your rifle — a Lee Enfield .303 — clean at all times. Dirt and mud could clog it up, making it ineffective in combat. Each soldier was issued with a long cord to clean the barrel and at one end was a piece of oil-soaked flannel called the four-by-two. Keeping your rifle clean in a filthy, muddy trench was difficult, so some soldiers tied an empty sandbag over the muzzle to keep out the mud.

Braces

Right ammunition pouches

Belt

Entrenching tool

Water bottle

Rifle

Left ammunition pouches

A soldier ready for inspection!

"It is particularly 'warm' on account of us being only 40 yards from the Germans. There is very little rifle fire but mostly hand grenades and trench mortars are used."

A SOLDIER DESCRIBES LIFE ACROSS A NARROW STRIP OF NO MAN'S LAND.

Rifle

Knapsack

Bayonet

Water Bottle

Entrenching tool

Entrenching tool handle

Inspections

After breakfast came the daily inspection by the platoon officer and sergeant. They would inspect your uniform and rifle. Sometimes they would inspect your feet for any signs of trench foot (see page 16). After this, the corporal would hand out the daily tasks and chores. Just before dark, there was the evening 'stand-to' – again you would stand on the fire-step with fixed bayonet. The corporal might take a roll call to make sure everyone was 'present and correct'.

Listening

One of the most unpopular duties at night was to be sent into the listening post. This was a narrow trench, or sap, going out into no man's land and you were expected to listen and report on enemy activity. Men hated it because in the winter it was freezing, boring and very dangerous. If the enemy attacked, those in the listening post would be the first to be killed.

The cloth strips round his legs are called 'puttees' and are designed to give his legs support while marching.

Hard Work

Combat took up a small proportion of a soldier's stay at the front. Most of the time he would carry out heavy manual work. There were always jobs that needed to be done in the trenches.

Like camels

Probably the most common chore was carrying, and men often complained they were more like camels than soldiers! Carrying heavy boxes of ammunition, water containers and food rations through the maze of muddy trenches was incredibly difficult and tiring. The troops gave names to the trenches – High Street, London Road and Piccadilly – but if you were not familiar with your sector, it was very easy to get lost, especially in the dark.

"At one period we had to commence work at 2am, we were supposed to rest in the day but we could not get any."

A SOLDIER DESCRIBES HOW GETTING SLEEP IN THE FRONT LINE WAS NOT EASY.

Looking after the trench

Trenches themselves needed constant attention. Water that flooded in had to be pumped out, sandbags had to be filled with earth and trench sides had to be constantly maintained. To make it easier to walk in these muddy holes, wooden duckboards were laid on the floor and these often had to be mended or replaced.

Stay awake!

At the front there was always sentry duty, which usually consisted of a two-hour watch, when soldiers had to keep a lookout for enemy raids or attacks. It was very important not to fall asleep during this crucial job because the punishment was execution by firing squad. If your chores were finished, you were allowed time to write home to loved ones, clean your rifle, mend your uniform or catch up on some precious sleep.

Wiring parties

An important part of each trench sector was the barbed wire placed in front of the fire trench, and that too had to be carefully maintained. Shelling could damage and blow holes in it. At night, wiring parties went out and drove wooden posts or screwed iron spirals (called picquets) into the ground that supported the rolls of barbed wire. They also replaced the broken sections.

Xmas Greetings and Best Wishes for the New Year From Pte J. Schneider

A Christmas and New Year card from the front.

A section of men practising going 'over the top'. Note the iron picquets in the barbed wire.

Food and Water

Naturally, food was very important to front-line troops and it can safely be said that there was never enough! The men carried out a lot of physical work, so British dieticians calculated that each soldier needed 3,574 calories a day. However, some experts agreed with the complaining troops that this was not enough.

Conditions behind the lines could be quite civilized, as seen in this soldiers' hut.

Knife, fork, spoon and cup

Grocery rations

Biscuits

Meat lozenges

Biscuits

Grocery rations

Bully beef

A soldier's kit list shows the rations that were carried by all men.

Rations

Food was known as rations and there were different types. Wet rations were porridge, soup, tea, bacon – anything that was cooked. Dry rations consisted of bread, hard biscuits, bully-beef (corned beef), cheese and butter – anything eaten cold. Iron rations were very special and only for use in emergencies. They were usually a tin of bully-beef, tea, sugar and biscuits and were never to be opened unless an officer gave permission. The Maconochie tin was an addition some men enjoyed. It contained sliced vegetables in a thin soup. Warmed up, it was acceptable, but cold, it was disgusting.

Drinking water

Water was always in short supply and had to be guarded carefully. It was carried by hand to the front line in petrol cans, and distributed in buckets to the men's water bottles. When water was scarce, men were tempted to fetch water from shell holes full of rain water. This was dangerous, as the water was often stagnant and contaminated, and a major cause of dysentery.

Treats for the Tommies (British soldiers)!
The Salvation Army making doughnuts for the troops.

British Tommies serve stew in the front line.

Jam for all!

The British Army provided mobile kitchens that tried to get as near to the front line as possible, where they prepared hot food in two huge metal cooking pots. If food did reach the men at the front, sent in hay-lined boxes, it was usually cold. The choice of food was limited, monotonous and nearly always stale. Jam was a source of annoyance for the troops, as all they got was plum and apple and nothing else!

"Our food consists of half a loaf of bread a day, bacon and tea for breakfast, bully-beef and biscuits for dinner, jam and cheese for tea."

A SOLDIER WRITING HOME IN 1915.

Trench Hygiene

Living in holes in the ground was not the healthiest life and trenches were particularly filthy places. Both Belgium and northern France have high levels of rainfall, especially in the winter.

Looking after feet

Living in mud-filled trenches gave rise to trench foot. This was a serious infection caused by permanent damp and cold conditions. Feet received poor blood supply and began to decay. Unless they were treated, gangrene set in which could lead to amputations. Trench foot was avoided by drying the feet daily, changing socks and smearing the feet with whale oil. Officers regularly inspected the feet of their platoon members.

"...the troops were in such a bad condition that the doctor sent in a report saying we were not fit for the line."

A TOMMY'S LETTER SHOWS HOW POOR CONDITIONS IN THE TRENCHES TOOK THEIR TOLL ON THE MEN.

The platoon leader inspects his men's feet. Trench foot was a serious problem and if men were hospitalized they could not fight.

Death and burial

Life in the trenches was dangerous. Soldiers new to the trenches would often fall victim to snipers, and almost constant shelling and artillery barrages meant that the casualty numbers were incredibly high. Difficult conditions made it hard to treat the wounded and to cope with the number of dead bodies. Men often had to bury their comrades as well as they could, but sometimes this was not possible. Often it was too dangerous to retrieve or bury dead comrades, so they had to be left where they fell.

Furry friends

Probably the most unpleasant aspect of trench life was the rats. They were everywhere and ate everything. They thrived on the vast number of dead bodies and food remains lying around the front. Some other unwelcome guests were body lice. They lived and laid eggs in the seams of clothes and covered the victim's body with bites. They itched terribly and if a man scratched them with dirty nails they became infected. Worst of all, the lice spread trench fever. A soldier infected with lice would be seen crushing the lice with his fingers or popping the eggs in his shirt seams with a candle.

Toilets

Toilets, or latrines, were very basic. A narrow trench was dug back from the parados and a deep hole dug. Wooden planks with holes in were placed over it. When it filled up it was covered with earth and another one dug. The smell, especially in hot weather, was appalling and it attracted flies. Despite being screened with corrugated iron sheets, latrines could be seen by enemy snipers and artillery. Some men preferred to use their tin helmets and throw the waste into no man's land!

No.S.C.40-A.   Headquarters Ferozepore Brigade
                17th June 1915.

To
    The Officer Commanding, Connaught Rangers,
        "   "   1/4th London Regt.
        "   "   89th Punjabis,
        "   "   129th Baluchis,
        "   "   57th Rifles.

1.   I am directed to say that the General Officer Commanding realizes that Battalions in the trenches have done a lot towards cleaning up the ground in their areas and in improving the sanitation but he considers that still more requires to be done.   The more important points he wishes taken in hand are the latrines and rubbish.

2.   Proper latrines must be dug, preferably leading off communication trenches, or at all events, some distance behind the front Trenches.   Excreta must never be left so that flies can get at it, but be covered over immediately with earth.

3.   All tins, rubbish, and remains of food must be buried daily.

4.   Drinking water in buckets, etc., must always be kept covered up.

Instructions for cleanliness in the trenches. These were incredibly difficult to enforce, especially when it rained.

'Put a Sock in it!'

Large numbers of men crowded into cramped, dirty and insanitary trenches was very stressful. This was made worse by sleep deprivation – lack of sleep. When people suffer from this, they become bad-tempered, run-down and cannot perform their duties as efficiently as they should.

Some soldiers cut space in the side of the trench to get some protection from the weather.

Sleepless nights

Why was it so uncomfortable in the front line? First of all, you had to sleep out of doors in all weathers and wear the same clothes for about five weeks. Officers had dug-outs with furniture, but ordinary soldiers had to make the best of the trench. Some slept on the fire step, others cut 'funk-holes' in the side of the trench for shelter. Secondly, there was constant noise. In a busy sector, artillery shells exploded all hours of the day and night. Sleep was difficult and at best, intermittent.

Catching cold

The most serious effect of the lack of sleep was the damage done to the body's immune system. As a result, soldiers easily picked up colds, chest infections, boils, toothache and abscesses.

A warm fire

Keeping warm in the winter was difficult. Braziers were brought in and men also made their own by puncturing the sides of an old bucket. Bags of fuel were carried to the front line, but once they were used up, men started taking wood from the trenches to burn. One advantage of the brazier was that food could be cooked on it if you did not have a tommy cooker. This was a little tin stove that could be use to boil water for tea or to cook bacon.

Essential equipment!
For that important cup of tea.

18

What a stink!

The noise, lack of sleep and the dirt were all made worse by the many disgusting smells in the trenches. Decomposing bodies, the latrines and the smell of your unwashed comrades pushed men's patience to the limit. Tempers snapped and anyone talking too loudly or too much was quickly told to, "Put a sock in it!"

An illustration of the cramped conditions of front-line trenches.

"When I was in the Somme district I had a really rough time, was nearly worked to death and had very little sleep."

LETTER FROM SOLDIER A. SMITH.

Trench Raid!

Raids were a very important part of life in the front line. Night-time raids on German positions were encouraged by the High Command for a number of reasons. They were designed to keep men 'on their toes' so they did not get used to the drudgery of trench warfare, or the quiet life. It was also hoped that frequent raids would instil an aggressive spirit in front-line troops.

        2nd Bde to 1st Cdn. Div.
Following message received from O.C. 8th Bn.
Section 2.
Begins. Have just returned from reconnaissance
with Kirkaldy. We went along ridge to support
48th Highlanders in S.W. corner D.1.c. 48th and
5th Royals were holding line 700 yards in original
front trench then bends back to L judge about
Cross Roads in C.6.b. Houses just North and North
West of this point must he occupied by Germans as
we got snipers enfilade fire from that direction.
Reserve 48th Highlanders Hqrs is in ST. JULIEN.
7th Bn. about C.12.b. German shells were falling
in road C.12.b. apparently coming from North.
German line appears to be from C.6.a. to Wood
C.10.d. All quiet in my front. Visited artillery
observation station in North East corner D.7.d.
is empty. Arranged disposition of 7th company in
locality "C" in case northern flank 3rd Bde was
pushed in. Message ends.

An extract from a trench message recording a reconnaissance raid to spy out the enemy. 'Enfilade fire' means dangerous crossfire.

Who goes?

A company or platoon commander would ask for volunteers for a raid and the men were carefully picked. Married men with children were rejected, as were men who had recently been in action. A small team of five to eight men was chosen, led by a junior officer.

What were the raids for?

The main aim of raids was to get information. What enemy regiment is in the opposite trench? Are they new to the sector? What are their defences like? Every raid would try to bring back German prisoners to be interrogated. A raid was more likely to succeed with quiet and surprise. Because of this, men preferred to leave rifles behind and take their own weapons like coshes, knives and knuckle-dusters.

A dangerous mission

Every man had his job. One would cut the wire and act as a guide for the return, one would carry a bayonet, others took Mills bombs (hand grenades) to drop in the trench and one would try to grab a prisoner. The men smeared their faces with mud and silently climbed into no man's land…

Sometimes the raids were successful and frightened prisoners were dragged back to the British lines. Sometimes the raiding party was caught by a German one. Then perhaps only one or two would return…

"We have been in action 24 days consecutively and don't know how long we can keep it up."

PLATOON SERGEANT 'BILLY', JULY 1915.

American troops stealthily work their way through the barbed wire.

Casualties

When the war broke out in 1914, it was estimated that Britain would need 50,000 beds for the expected casualties. By Christmas, 73,000 wounded had been sent back to Britain for treatment. As the fighting dragged on, medical services became a crucial part of the war effort.

Wounds and gas

What sort of injuries happened to front-line soldiers? The majority came from bullets, artillery and the effects of poison gas. The Germans first used gas in 1915 and Britain and France soon followed. This was the first example of chemical weapons in warfare. Gas killed nearly 6,000 British troops. The different types of gas caused blisters, blinding and severe respiratory damage. Gas masks became an important feature of the front line, as did the 'Gas Alert!' signs.

Front-line troops with the Gas Alert 'On'.

"I must have breathed in enough gas to put me out of action...I was sent to the Casualty Clearing Station on August 3rd and reached Rouen Hospital the next day...crossed the Channel on a splendid boat with every convenience."

A GASSED SOLDIER TELLS OF HIS QUICK TREATMENT.

Shell shock

The constant artillery bombardments caused both physical and mental damage. Lumps of red hot metal caused terrible wounds, but sometimes the strain of intense shell explosions led to shell shock – known today as Post Traumatic Stress Disorder. Trenches collapsed in these massive bombardments and men were often buried alive.

No peeking!

When men first entered the trenches they were tempted to peep over the parapet and many were killed or wounded by snipers. In fact, trench warfare resulted in a huge number of face and head wounds and the tin helmet became a crucial piece of equipment. So too did the trench periscope, which allowed men to safely study no man's land.

Treating the wounded

What happened to wounded soldiers? If they could not walk, stretcher bearers took them to a Regimental Aid Post (RAP) where their wounds were patched up. They were then taken to an Advanced Dressing Station where a medical officer assessed the soldier's condition.

Thousands of women volunteered to join the numerous hospitals in France and Belgium.

If the medical officer assessed that the soldier was dying and could not be saved, then he was made comfortable. The wounded were graded according to severity. A white label meant non-serious and a red and white label meant urgent enough to return to Britain. Even minor wounds could become fatally infected as there were no antibiotics to treat them.

One of the well-equipped hospital trains.

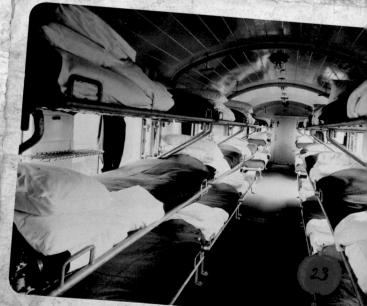

23

Danger: Above and Below

Anywhere in the front line was risky, but two jobs stand out as especially dangerous: trench runners and miners or sappers.

Runners

Communication in and out of the trenches was very important. The signallers set up telegraph and telephone lines but they were often damaged by artillery. Homing pigeons were used, but were not always reliable. Therefore, trench runners were important in carrying messages between platoons and company headquarters, or from company to battalion headquarters. They were recognized by a red ribbon pinned to their arms and were supposed to work in pairs in case of injury. However, there was such a shortage of runners that they tended to work on their own.

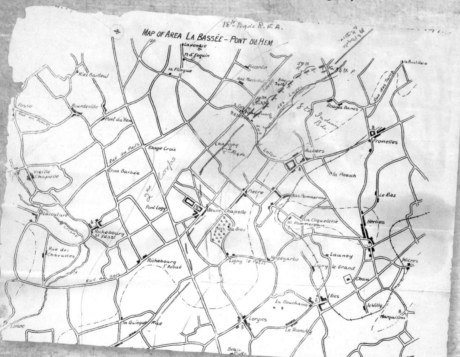

Trench runners had to memorize positions of trenches, roads and artillery batteries when taking messages to and from Brigade Headquarters.

Although runners were exempted from certain duties – some parades and manual labour – their job was very hazardous. They had to leave the safety of below ground and dodge artillery shells, machine-gun and rifle fire, gas and flooded trenches. Experienced runners got to know their trench network well, but it might take five hours to carry a message a relatively short distance. Casualty rates were high.

Sappers

Both sides dug mines underneath each other's trenches that would be filled with explosives and blown up. The Army even brought in skilled miners from the British coalfields. It was dangerous work. They could often hear the opposing force working nearby. Sometimes they dug into each other's tunnels and desperate fighting took place in the dark. There were cave-ins and miners were also overcome with gas seeping from the moved earth. Canaries were brought in to detect gas. The birds would stop singing and die if there was gas in the air.

Mines were dug to coincide with big attacks and the explosions marked the start of battles such as the Somme (1916) and Messines (1917). Large amounts of explosives (ammonal) were placed at the end of the tunnel and blocked off by sandbags so that the blast would go upwards. It was hoped they would cause a breakthrough in the enemy line, but they never succeeded.

Sapper FH Ferdinand had one of the toughest jobs on the Western Front.

"We were welcomed by a big dose of gas shells and shrapnel, which was applied throughout the night by the German artillery."

IT WAS THESE SORT OF BARRAGES THAT MADE THE JOB OF A TRENCH RUNNER SO DANGEROUS.

The Big Push

When the Germans occupied parts of Belgium and France in 1914, the Allies were constantly trying to push them back over the border. The Germans knew this and built strong, deep trenches. Unfortunately, the machine gun gave the advantage to the defender, which meant that dislodging the Germans was always going to be difficult.

German tactics

To make matters worse, the Germans used concrete in their defences. They built strong points and pillboxes for their machine guns and deep underground shelters to protect their soldiers from artillery. Despite all this, the British generals believed in breakthrough tactics, or big pushes, and attempted to smash through German defences and into open space behind their lines. This tactic had not worked at Loos in 1915, but the British tried again in 1916 on the Somme.

A cartoon poster designed to discourage workers from taking their holidays so shell production was maintained.

Reproduced by the Special Permission of the Proprietors of "Punch."

THE BIG PUSH.

MUNITION WORKER. "WELL, I'M NOT TAKING A HOLIDAY MYSELF JUST YET, BUT I'M SENDING THESE KIDS OF MINE FOR A LITTLE TRIP ON THE CONTINENT."

Preparing for battle

For the troops involved it was a very tense time. They did not like their normal routine being disturbed. There were practice attacks behind the lines when Generals, know as 'brass hats', turned up and watched the men in full kit run towards tapes that represented enemy trenches. There was much hanging around, boredom and speeches and they were glad when it was all over. Some men began to get 'windy' or scared.

GERMAN TRENCHES
On the WESTERN FRONT.
(1) BEFORE BOMBARDMENT.

An aerial photograph showing German trenches before a bombardment.

The same area after the bombardment. Again, these pictures were to encourage workers not to take their holidays.

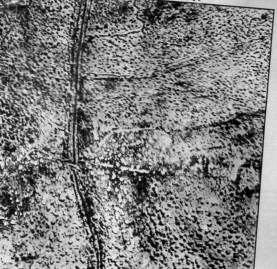

(2) AFTER BOMBARDMENT.

MUNITION WORKERS - SEE THE EFFECT - OF YOUR WORK!
POSTPONE YOUR HOLIDAYS AND PILE UP THE SHELLS.

The battle

On 23 June 1916, an eight-day artillery barrage was unleashed against the German defences. Unfortunately, the British fired shrapnel shells, which only jumbled up the German wire without breaking it. The shells just scratched the surface, while the Germans sheltered safely in their bunkers 12 metres underground.

On 1 July, 750,000 British troops walked across no man's land to take the German trenches. However, the defenders rushed up from their bunkers unharmed, set up their machine guns and mowed down the advancing British troops. 56,000 were wounded on the first day and a third of them died. The battle dragged on until November.

"My goodness, what a reception the Huns had in store for us, they simply swept the ground with machine-gun fire and shrapnel."

A SOLDIER'S LETTER TO HIS MOTHER, MAY 1916.

Behind the Lines

When a company was told it was going out
of the line for a rest, morale increased immediately.
The men's thoughts turned to the little luxuries
and good times they were going to have. As the relieving
troops arrived, they asked: "What's it like here?" "Cushy
enough", was always
the reply.

Sleep

A company would arrive in
the town where it was to be
billeted in a very bedraggled
state. The men may have
been placed in houses, barns,
stables, or possibly tents in a
camp. If it was evening some
would sleep immediately.
Soldiers coming out of the
line were often so exhausted
that they might sleep for
14 hours.

**When there was not enough
room in houses or billets,
tent camps were set up for
the men.**

A change of scene

The men in the billets had to fend for themselves, while others were placed in homes
with families. After overcoming embarrassment – not many spoke French – the men
settled into family life, but it was a reminder of what they were missing at home.
   To the men, everything looked so colourful compared to the brown, drab muddy
trenches they had lived in for five weeks. Behind the lines they would see greens,
yellows, reds, blues and even civilians! Life was worth living.

"We are billeted in a barn and have a sea of mud to get through. We have no beds, so sleep on the ground, fires are not allowed and at night it is devilish cold."

A NOT-SO-LUCKY SOLDIER WRITES HOME IN FEBRUARY 1916.

Soldiers rarely sang on their way up to the line, but marching out of it they enthusiastically sang their songs:

"Rolling home, Rolling home... By the light of the silvery mo-oo-on!

Happy is the day when you draw your buckshee pay. And you're rolling, rolling, rolling, rolling home."

Wash time

Next morning the men went straight to the baths. This was essential because they were all 'lousy'. They handed in their towel, socks, shirt and underpants and received clean ones. Bath-houses were often breweries and the large vats were used for bathing. Some even had showers. The men splashed, soaped themselves and mucked around. It felt good to be clean!

'At ease!' A group of soldiers have deserved rest far away from the fighting.

Time Off

A typical day behind the lines…

First up: getting paid! The company assembles and forms a semi-circle round a table where the captain, an officer and the quarter-master sergeant sit.

After the sergeants have been paid, the men are called up alphabetically. We each salute and take off our caps. This is important. If the captain does not think we have had a proper haircut the day before, after the baths — no pay! The men do not like closely cropped hair, but there is a reason for it. In case of a head wound, matted hair with dried blood will make the dressing of wounds more difficult and time consuming.

With pay in our pockets we walk around the town looking for things to spend it on. The most popular place is the estaminet — a cross between a bar, café and private house. The men call them 'just-a-minutes' and they are an essential home from home. Usually, they are family run, the father cooks, the mother (Madame) is in charge and the daughters serve the food. Eggs and 'pommes frites' (chips) is the most popular meal and weak beer, 'vin blong' (white wine), coffee, soup, ham, sausages and omelettes are all available. They are warm, welcoming places and their importance to us war-weary soldiers should not be underestimated.

Some Tommies relax with French soldiers and civilians at a local Estaminet.

The estaminet

The atmosphere in an estaminet was free and easy, people could smoke, drink, chat and have a good sing-song. You could have brandy, but as spirits were only available to officers, it was usually served in the coffee. However, if Madame thought you were getting too noisy or rowdy, you were shown the door!

"We left the trenches at Vimy Ridge on July 5th and marching back about 14 miles we eventually reached a village named Ostreville for the purpose of a Divisional rest!"

ONE TOMMY DESCRIBES LEAVING THE TRENCHES FOR A REST.

The Locals

It was very important that the British Army got on well with French and Belgian civilians. Great efforts were made to make sure the relationship was friendly. Military police (redcaps) patrolled the billeted areas and watched out for drunken and rowdy behaviour which could upset local people.

Goods for sale

For a population whose livelihood had been ruined by the war, the presence of large numbers of soldiers with pay to spend was a great opportunity to make money. Civilians provided goods and services for the Tommies. Cottages on the side of roads would have a sign saying *cafe au lait* (white coffee) and an open door. It was even known for families to invite groups of soldiers into their homes for coffee and refuse payment.

Arguments

When troops knew they were going back to the front, women came out selling food, saying; "*Oranges pour les trenches*" or "*Oeufs pour les trenches*" (meaning oranges or eggs for the trenches). The Tommies got upset when locals charged unfairly high prices. The British soldier was not paid a lot, 1 shilling (5p) a day, and there were unpleasant arguments when it was thought the locals took advantage. Civilians became angry when troops stole chickens, eggs, vegetables and fruit from their gardens and farms.

Organising a kitty

Apart from the food for sale in the estaminets, some soldiers grouped together and elected a mess secretary to organize marvellous meals. His job was to collect a kitty (each man would contribute a few francs) and, perhaps because he spoke a little French, he would go to the woman of the house and ask if she could buy some food from the local market. She would then cook a dinner once a day for the men and be paid for her trouble. These arrangements worked very well and the quality of food was excellent. Sweet omelettes were popular, with strawberry jam, not apple and plum!

"We were about to bivouac (put up tents) in an orchard but an old Frenchman appeared on the scene and raised objections...thinking that we would wander about his place!"

A LETTER HOME SHOWS THE TENSION BETWEEN THE SOLDIERS AND LOCALS.

This cartoon shows a Tommy trying out his French phrases at the estaminet. Madame is not impressed.

Discipline

The disciplinary code of the British Army was both complicated and harsh. Soldiers could be in trouble for many reasons, from being dirty on parade to failing to salute an officer.

Committing a crime

If the crime was relatively minor, you were placed 'on a charge' and appeared before your company commander. The sergeant would read out the charge and the punishment was usually an unpleasant job like filling in the latrines. More serious crimes involved a 'court martial' which was heard by high-ranking officers. The crimes they dealt with were drunkenness, desertion, rudeness to officers, loss or damage of Army property and absence without permission. A 'soldier's friend' could help defend the accused, but the conviction rates in these courts was high – 89 per cent.

Photograph of a group of ten Australian deserters which was sent to the A.P.M. Havre, with the following letter:–

"Sir,   With all due respect we send you this P.C. as a souvenir trusting that you will keep it as a mark of esteem from those who know you well. At the same time trusting that Nous jamais regardez vous encore.   Au revoir.   Nous"

Information regarding any of these men should be addressed to Provost Marshal, G.H.Q., reference his No. M/4292/924 (see "KI-" given in P.G. No.19 para. A.l.)

Australian deserters tell the Assistant Provost Marshal (head of the military police) that they won't ever see him again!

Deliberate injuries

Another serious crime was the 'self-inflicted wound' (SIW). Some men, pushed to the limits of endurance by the war, injured themselves deliberately to get out of the trenches. The most common method was to shoot themselves in the hand or foot. 3,894 men were convicted of SIWs and although none were executed, they all went to prison.

Punishments

Punishments varied from imprisonment or fines, to demotion (reduction in rank) or even death. 346 men were executed during the war, mainly for desertion (246), but also for murder, leaving their post, sleeping on duty and throwing away their weapons. A well-known and widespread punishment for serious crimes was 'Field Punishment No.1'. This involved a man being chained to a wheel or wooden frame for up to two hours a day.

The Workers' Union complains about the humiliation and degradation of Field Punishment No. 1.

Field Punishment No. 1 was used over 60,000 times during World War I.

"One fine evening, with a big crowd all set for a game (of bingo), two military policemen appeared with a handcuffed prisoner and, in full view of the crowd and the villagers, tied him to the wheel of a limber, cruciform fashion. The poor devil, a British Tommy, was undergoing Field Punishment No. 1, and this public exposure was a part of the punishment..."

GEORGE COPPARD, WITH A MACHINE GUN TO CAMBRAI, 1968.

The main aim was public humiliation, which made it unpopular with the men. Less well known is that victims were also given the worst jobs to carry out and they fell to the bottom of the list for men going on leave. Interestingly, discipline in the Australian and Canadian Armies was much more relaxed and it was known for Australian soldiers on finding soldiers tied to a wheel to simply release them!

Trench Humour

Because of the intense stress and strain of trench warfare, soldiers turned to humour as a way of coping. A typical mind-set of many Tommies was to grumble when things went well and joke when things were bad. Many humorous newspapers and magazines were produced by British, Canadian, Australian and New Zealand soldiers. They poked fun at the idiocy of war, the officers in charge and the Army's rules and regulations.

⊙ THE ⊙ WIPERS TIMES.
OR
SALIENT NEWS.

No 1. Vol. 1.   Saturday, 12th February, 1916.   PRICE 20 FRANCS

WIPERS FISH-HOOK & MENIN RAILWAY.
—o—
DAILY EXCURSION TICKETS ARE ISSUED TO

MENIN.

TRAINS WILL LEAVE DAILY AT 8 A.M. & 1 P.M., COMMENCING FEB 1st, 1916. FOR FURTHER PARTICULARS SEE SMALL BILLS.

Until further notice trains will not go beyond Gordon Farm Station, line beyond that closed for alterations.

UNDER ENTIRELY NEW MANAGEMENT.
—o—
HOTEL DES RAMPARTS.
—o—
NO EXPENSE HAS BEEN SPARED BY THE NEW MANAGEMENT IN THE RE-DECORATING AND RE-FITTING OF THIS FIRST-CLASS HOTEL.

SPECIALLY RECOMMENDED TO BUSINESS MEN.

New Electric Installation.   5 Private Lines. Tel Pioneers, Ypres.

Wipers Times

The most famous and unusual of the trench newspapers was the *Wipers Times*, first published in 1916. Its name came from the British pronunciation of the Belgian town of Ypres. It was unusual because it was printed very close to the front-line fighting. Ypres was at the centre of the Ypres Salient, the worst part of the British front line. The Salient pushed into the enemy's front so the Germans attacked it from three sides. The town was virtually destroyed by German artillery and British casualties were huge. In the regular column 'Things We Want to Know' (16 February 1916) the paper asked: "1. Who discovered the Salient? 2. Why?"

The cover of the very first edition of The Wipers Times. The joke about 'The Hotel Des Ramparts' is that the town of Ypres was a pile of rubble because of German shelling!

Keeping the Germans guessing

The paper changed titles a number of times to keep the Germans guessing. It became the *New Church Times*, the *Kemmel Times*, the *Somme Times* and the *Better Times*. One item helpfully displayed the weather probability: "5:1 Mist, 11:2 East Wind or Frost, 8:1 Chloride" (poison gas!).

"The printing works were a matter of 50 yards or so down the road, and there was an issue of the paper nearly completed. We did not stay to finish it."

THE EDITOR OF THE *WIPERS TIMES* DESCRIBES THE PROBLEMS TRYING TO PUBLISH DURING THE GERMAN SPRING OFFENSIVE, 1918.

XXᵗʰ "LIGHT" DIVISION

A FEW DAYS' REST IN BILLETS

BILLET 41
2 Officers
8 men

JANUARY 1917

A cartoon makes fun of the conditions in the billets.

Making fun

One spoof letter poked fun at the civilian obsession with sending the troops things they did not need. A charity begs funds for pyjamas: *"We hear…that poor fellows… only have one pair in the trenches."*

The feature 'News from the Ration Dump' regularly reported — and ridiculed — the latest crazy rumours that swept through the trenches: *"Leave is about to re-open on the Western Front. The Germans are short of shells. The Germans have no guns. The British and French Cavalry swam the Rhine last night near Cologne and are now…in the suburbs of Berlin."*

Entertainment

The authorities were keen to provide entertainment and activities for the troops resting out of the line. They feared boredom would lead to excessive drinking and rowdy behaviour. Some towns had plenty going on, while other villages were much quieter.

What a show!

Concert parties circulated, putting on plays. These were mostly humorous, revues, called 'follies', pantomimes and variety shows. As women were not allowed near the front, there was a demand for female impersonators, or Dames, as they were called. One group was caught up in the German spring offensive in March 1918 and had to escape, leaving all their costumes behind.

The Music Hall had been so popular pre-1914 that similar entertainment was put on for the men behind the line.

Team games

Sport was another popular activity for troops at rest. Football was closely followed by players and spectators. Most competitions took place between platoons, and the rivalry was fierce. Knock-out competitions were well attended and titles won. Cricket was played, although it tended to be more popular with officers. The condition of pitches varied, making some bowling deliveries as dangerous as the German artillery!

The men were quick to spot an opportunity for sport. When ponds or lakes froze, ice hockey matches were played with walking sticks. With so many horses on the Western Front, horse shows and races were common. In summer, Divisional sports days were held consisting of athletic events, sack races and even bike races. It was an opportunity for men and officers to have a good time and bet on the events!

A troupe of entertainers known as 'Pierrots' and the football team of the 11th Hussars.

Post!

Everyone looked forward to the post. Letters and parcels were distributed by the company headquarters office. Eager faces smiled when their names were called and letters and parcels were thrown at them to catch. Best were the parcels containing food, socks and most important, candles. Many precious objects were hidden in a scraped out loaf of bread!

No 87760. L. Cpl. A. Smith. R.E.,
3rd Corps Railhead,
B. E. F.
France.
August 3rd 1915.

Dear Sir, I was very glad to get your letter some weeks ago. It is always nice to get some Office news out here. I was glad to hear that Hull & Kemball had been promoted to Cpls.

A SOLDIER'S LETTER FROM FRANCE, 1915.

"I was very glad to get your letter some weeks ago. It is always nice to get some Office news out here."

Soldiers were always glad to receive post and to hear the news from home.

Prisoners of War

Another way that troops left the trenches was by being captured and made Prisoners of War (POWs). About 185,000 British POWs were held in German camps.

Poor camps

The quality of German camps varied enormously. Some were very badly run and prisoners treated harshly. At Wittenberg, during 1914–15, the camp authorities allowed an outbreak of typhus to get out of control. With little running water or soap and prisoners forced to sleep three to a mattress, the disease spread quickly. Out of nearly 2,000 cases, 185 died. After the epidemic, the commandant brought in guard dogs, failed to distribute enough overcoats and did not pay the prisoners fully for their work. He was replaced and soon conditions at Wittenberg improved.

British and French prisoners arrive at a POW camp. By 1916, Germany was short of food, so conditions were harsh.

Better camps

Other camps, such as Parchim and Soltau, had better reputations. Here, food parcels from the British Central Prisoners of War Committee got through to the prisoners regularly and the quality of the food was acceptable although not plentiful. Washing facilities, accommodation, medical care, lessons and shops were available and wounded prisoners received care for their injuries.

By the end of 1918, British POWs had been sent 9 million food parcels and 800,000 clothing parcels from home!

Different experiences

For the vast majority of prisoners, the biggest challenge was boredom. In time, sports were organised when equipment for football, rugby, tennis and boxing started arriving. Even the camp authorities realized that games raised morale and improved the health of prisoners. However, many prisoners had terrible experiences and there were many cases of malnutrition and exhaustion. Guards or commandants who had forced POWs to work in coal mines, or presided over filthy camp conditions, were put on trial.

CHARLES MAYO WAS WOUNDED AND CAPTURED IN 1915. HIS LETTERS TALK OF SHORTAGES AND REQUESTS FOR ITEMS:

"two sheets for a single bed...a couple of towels and some soap... and bread...Apologies for another begging letter... Your loving son, Charlie."

Football matches were very popular in the camps and were well attended.

The End of Trench Warfare

In the spring of 1918, the Germans made a last desperate attempt to win the war. Operation Michael (21 March) was designed to deliver a killer blow to the British 5th Army. It failed. Other attacks were launched in April and May, but by June all the offensives had stalled. What would happen next?

The Mark IV tank was Britain's most effective tank during the second half of the war. Advancing troops could take cover behind it.

The German retreat

Successful Allied attacks in July and August put the Germans on the defensive. The breakthrough came on 8 August, when Australian and Canadian troops, spearheaded by new tanks, smashed their way into German territory. From this moment the German Armies were in retreat. General Ludendorff called 8 August 'the black day of the German Army in the war'. By the end of September the formidable Hindenburg Line had been breached. The fall of this network of deep concrete fortifications and trench-works was a massive blow. From then on, the war was fought on open ground not in trenches.

Out of the trenches

For the troops this was a strange experience. They felt awkward with no fire-steps or parapets to protect them. When the machine-gun bullets flew, they had to take cover behind anything they could find. The battlefield was a desolate sight that damp autumn – smashed cottages, burned churches, starving civilians, corpses, dead horses, and all the waste and equipment abandoned by a retreating Army.

> "The sights and smells are awful, as a good many of the chaps lay just as they fell during the advance. It was impossible to bury them."
>
> A TOMMY DESCRIBES THE REALITY OF WAR.

British troops walk through the devastation of the Western Front.

Open warfare

For the British Army this open warfare was costly, and in the last three months of the war it suffered over a quarter of a million casualties. However, the German Army was collapsing and its leaders agreed to an armistice at 11am on 11 November 1918. When this was announced to the men, some officers could not believe how calmly they took the news.

"The war is over."

Some raised a feeble *"Oo-ray"*.

Everyone had had enough...

Peace Celebrations, London, 19 July 1919. The Cenotaph was built of wood and plaster for the occasion and later rebuilt in stone.

The Battlefields Today

Many people visit the old battlefields of the Western Front. Some are interested in the history, others are curious and stop on their drive back from a continental holiday. Many see it as a type of pilgrimage – perhaps to visit the grave of a relative, while others go in order to pay their respects to the generation who gave up so much.

Cemeteries

If you go to the battlefields of Belgium and France today, the most common feature you will see are the cemeteries. Some are tiny. Others are vast, like Tyne Cot (below) near Passchendaele, which contains the graves of 11,908 soldiers. It is the largest Commonwealth war cemetery anywhere in the world. The cemeteries all contain white limestone headstones and the large Cross of Sacrifice. Each headstone is carved in the same font, showing the soldier's army corps or national emblem, name, rank and number. The inscription at the bottom was usually chosen by the family of the fallen soldier. If the soldier was unidentified, the stone carries an inscription chosen by the author Rudyard Kipling, 'Known Unto God'.

The War Graves Commission

These beautiful cemeteries are cared for by the Commonwealth War Graves Commission and costs are shared by the United Kingdom, Canadian, Australian, New Zealand, Indian and South African governments. The Commission cares for war graves not only in Belgium and France, but all around the world.

The trenches

Many visitors are interested in the preserved stretches of trenches that can be found along the old front line. Hill 62, near Ypres; Vimy Ridge, north of Arras; and Newfoundland Memorial Park near Albert, all allow you to walk down sections of old trenches.

A section of preserved trench at Vimy Ridge, near Arras, France. The duckboards and sandbags have been set in concrete.

First and last

For many, one of the most poignant places is the Symphorien British cemetery near Mons. Laid out like an English garden it contains the graves of the first and last men to die in the war. Private J. Parr of the Middlesex Regiment was killed on 21 August 1914. Private G.E. Ellison of the Royal Irish Lancers died on 11 November 1918 – the last day of the war.

Glossary

abscess an infected and swollen area of the skin

antibiotics medicine that can kill bacterial infections

armistice an agreement between two sides to stop fighting

battalion a unit of 1,007 soldiers, led by a lieutenant colonel

bayonet a short stabbing sword attached to the end of a rifle

billet temporary housing for soldiers, this could be a civilian's house, barn or stable

brazier a portable can for holding hot coals, to be used as a heater

breach a hole or gap made in an enemy line by advancing forces

calorie a unit of energy provided by food

company a unit of 227 soldiers, led by a major or captain

contaminated made something dirty or impure by mixing with a poisonous substance

corned-beef preserved beef, contained in tins. The British Army called it 'bully-beef'.

corporal a non-commissioned officer (NCO) in the Army, in charge of a section of 12 men

corps a branch of the military

cosh a thick or heavy stick used as a weapon

crisis a dangerous argument between countries

deserter someone who abandons their military post

duckboard a board used to make a path over muddy or wet ground, made from wooden slats joined together

dysentery a disease of the bowels, usually caused by dirty water

fortification a building or position that is strengthened against attack

galleries passages that were dug under the enemy's trenches

gangrene when a part of a person's body decays because of a lack of blood supply

interrogate when a person asks someone many questions in order to find out information

kitty a fund of money belonging to a group, that everyone contributes to

knuckle-duster a metal weapon slipped over the knuckles to increase the power of a punch

latrine a simple toilet, usually a hole in the ground

leave a period of time a soldier is allowed away from the fighting

lousy to be infected with lice

malnutrition weakness caused by not having enough food, or only having poor food

morale the amount of confidence or enthusiasm a group of people have during difficult or testing times

neutrality when a country is independent; not joined with another by an alliance

periscope a device by which a person can see things that are out of sight, usually a tube attached to a set of mirrors

pillbox a concrete strong point usually containing machine guns

platoon a unit of 52 soldiers led by a lieutenant

quarter-master sergeant the person in charge of supplying food and clothing for the soldiers

respiratory damage damage to the lungs

roll call like a register, calling out names to check who is present

round the military term for a bullet

sap a narrow trench leading out from the front or the rear of a main front-line trench

section a unit of 13 soldiers, led by a corporal

shell shock a condition of intense fear, brought on by artillery barrages. The term was not used until 1916.

sniper a rifleman, usually hidden, whose job was to shoot unsuspecting soldiers

stagnant having an unpleasant smell as a result of standing still

Tommy the nickname for a British soldier

trench foot a severe condition brought on by intense cold or damp. It could lead to gangrene and amputation.

typhus an infectious disease spread by lice

volunteer a person who joins the army through his or her own free will

Further Information

Books

Bravery in World War I (Beyond the Call of Duty)
by Peter Hicks, Wayland, 2013.

Brothers at War – A First World War Family History
by Sarah Ridley, Franklin Watts, 2013.

Men, Women and Children in the First World War
by Philip Steele, Wayland, 2013.

The Trenches, A First World War Soldier 1914-18 (My Story)
by Jim Eldridge, Scholastic, 2008.

The Usborne Introduction to the First World War
by Ruth Brocklehurst and Harry Brook, Usborne Publishing, 2007.

Websites

nationalarchives.gov.uk
nationalarchives.gov.uk/education/greatwar/
The website of The National Archives and the web address for their World War One education pages.

www.greatwar.co.uk
A guide to the battlefields and history of World War One.

www.spartacus.schoolnet.co.uk/FWW.htm
An encyclopaedia of World War One.

www.iwm.org.uk
Website of the Imperial War Museum with the latest information on the 1914 centenary.

www.nam.ac.uk
Website of the National Army Museum with a wealth of information about World War One.

Places to visit

The Imperial War Museum, London
A huge collection on both World Wars.

The National Army Museum, London
The history of the British Army from A-Z, including World War One.

In Flanders Fields Museum, Ypres, Belgium
Based in the renovated Cloth Hall, this superb museum tells you all about World War One in the Ypres Salient.

Musee des Abris, Albert, France
Everything you need to know about the Battle of the Somme, with artefacts and photographs on display.

Index